ONE NATION,

Wisdom

MADE IN AMERICA

Common Sense and Uncommon Genius
from Great Americans

ONE NATION,

Wisdom

MADE IN AMERICA

THE **POPULAR** GROUP

This book was written by Walnut Grove Press for exclusive use by the Popular Publishing Company.

Popular Publishing Company LLC
1700 Broadway
New York, NY 10019

ISBN 1-59027-069-X

The ideas expressed in this book are not, in all cases, exact quotations, as some have been edited for clarity and brevity. In all cases, the author has attempted to maintain the speaker's original intent. In some cases, material for this book was obtained from secondary sources, primarily print media. While every effort was made to ensure the accuracy of these sources, the accuracy cannot be guaranteed. For additions, deletions, corrections or clarifications in future editions of this text, please write Popular Publishing Company LLC.

Certain elements of this text, including quotations, stories, and selected groupings of Bible verses, have appeared, in part or in whole, in publications produced by Walnut Grove Press of Nashville, TN; these excerpts are used with permission.

Printed in the United States of America
Page Layout Design by Bart Dawson
Cover Design: Tiffany Berry

1 2 3 4 5 6 7 8 9 10 • 02 03 04 05 06 07 08 09 10

Table of Contents

merica…so much can be said about her: The world's great superpower. The land of opportunity. A grand experiment in democracy. The land of the free…the home of the brave. And, of course, for those of us who are blessed to live here, the greatest nation on earth.

This book is a collection of wisdom that is distinctly American. It tells a story of hope, courage, confidence, and self-reliance through the words of notable sons and daughters of the Good Old USA. On the pages that follow, readers will be reminded of the principles and values that have made, and continue to make, America unique among nations.

The foundation of America's greatness has many stones, but the cornerstone is freedom. The United States of America was founded upon the principle that its citizens would be free to pursue life, love, and happiness with the fewest possible constraints. This experiment in freedom has resulted in an explosion of creativity and commerce unequaled in the history of mankind. But, the freedoms we enjoy must never be taken for granted. The world remains a dangerous place, and liberties must be defended if they are to be preserved. Our generation of Americans, like every generation before it, must not only dream the American dream; we must also protect it.

If you happen to be a grateful niece or nephew

of Uncle Sam, say a word of thanks. While you're at it, take the time to consider the great ideas contained in this text. When you do, you'll discover a collection of intellectual treasures proudly adorned in red, white and blue: the combination of common-sense genius and wide-eyed optimism that is truly Wisdom Made in America.

Chapter 1

★★★★★

AMERICA

I do believe that America shall continue
to grow, to multiply, and to prosper until
we exhibit an association powerful, wise,
and happy beyond what has yet
been seen by men.

Thomas Jefferson

The American dream is alive and well. And, if you don't believe it, just ask the millions of hard-working men and women who seek to become American citizens. America remains a land of freedom, prosperity, and opportunity. It is a place where dreams can still come true for those who are willing to work hard and smart. It is still the world's greatest superpower, the world's greatest economic engine, and the world's greatest melting pot.

We Americans are blessed beyond measure. Of course, our nation is not perfect, but, it remains the least imperfect nation on earth. And, as grateful citizens, we must do our part to protect America and preserve her liberties just as surely as we work to create better lives for ourselves and our families.

I always consider the founding of America with reverence and wonder.

John Adams

One flag, one land, one heart, one hand, One Nation, evermore!

Oliver Wendell Holmes, Sr.

The promise of America is a simple promise: Every person shall share in the blessings of this land. And they shall share on the basis of their merits as individuals. They shall not be judged by their color or by their beliefs, or by their religion, or by where they were born, or the neighborhood in which they live.

Lyndon Baines Johnson

One Country, one Constitution, one Destiny.
Daniel Webster

America, because you build for mankind, I build for you.

Walt Whitman

We, here in America, hold in our hands the hope of the world.

Theodore Roosevelt

We highly resolve that this nation, under God, shall have a new birth of freedom, and that government of the people, by the people, for the people, shall not perish from the earth.

Abraham Lincoln

America is another name for opportunity. Our whole history appears like a last effort of divine providence on behalf of the human race.

Ralph Waldo Emerson

America is essentially a dream, a dream as yet unfulfilled. It is a dream of a land where men of all races, of all nationalities, and of all creeds can live together as brothers.

Martin Luther King, Jr.

There is nothing wrong with America that the faith, love of freedom, intelligence, and energy of her citizens cannot cure.

Dwight D. Eisenhower

America is a willingness of heart.

F. Scott Fitzgerald

If you take advantage of everything America has to offer, there's nothing you can't accomplish.

Geraldine Ferraro

The future belongs to those who believe in the beauty of their dreams.

Eleanor Roosevelt

What's right about America is that although we have a mess of problems, we have a great capacity, intellect, and resources to do something about them.

Henry Ford II

We become not a melting pot but a beautiful mosaic. Different people, different beliefs, different yearnings, different hopes, different dreams.

Jimmy Carter

Ours is the only country deliberately founded on a good idea.

John Gunther

★★★★★

On July 4, 1776, the Declaration of Independence was signed by John Hancock, the presiding officer of the Second Continental Congress, and by Charles Thompson, secretary. On August 2 of the same year, the other members of the Continental Congress signed a parchment copy of the document.

On July 4,1777, bonfires lit the night sky of Philadelphia, and church bells rang as the city's citizens celebrated their nation's first anniversary. The 4th of July soon became America's most important patriotic holiday, and it remains so today. On that day, we Americans light up the grills, ice down the cold drinks, and marvel at the fireworks. May we also pause to speak a word of thanks for the dual blessings of freedom and opportunity that comprise the bedrock and the foundation of the American Dream.

You have to love a nation that celebrates its independence every July 4th, not with a parade of guns, tanks, and soldiers who file by the White House in a show of strength and muscle, but with family picnics where kids throw Frisbees, the potato salad gets iffy, and the flies die from happiness. You may think you have overeaten, but it is patriotism.

Erma Bombeck

Chapter 2

★★★★★

FREEDOM

America is best described
by one word:
freedom.

Dwight D. Eisenhower

*A*dlai Stevenson once correctly observed, "America is much more than a geographical fact. It is a political and moral fact, the first community in which men set out in principle to institutionalize freedom, responsible government, and human equality." The United States of America serves as a shining example of freedom and tolerance. Americans are free to speak their minds and to chart their destinies with a minimum of interference from governmental powers. Americans are free to cast their votes without hindrance or reprisal. Citizens are free to worship God as they see fit and to educate themselves to the extent they choose. Indeed, America has earned its right to be called "The Land of the Free."

This generation, like every one that preceded it, must protect the liberties that are woven into the fabric of American society. Freedom, after all, is never really free; to endure, liberty must be earned again and again by citizens who seek to leave their nation just a little better than they found her.

Poet Carl Sandburg wrote, "Freedom is a habit." May we, as freedom-loving Americans, learn the habit well and teach it thoroughly to our children.

Freedom is the last, best hope of earth.

Abraham Lincoln

Everything that is really good and inspiring is created by individuals who labor in freedom.

Albert Einstein

The best energies of my life have been spent in endeavoring to establish and perpetuate the blessings of free government.

Andrew Johnson

You can only protect your liberties in this world by protecting the other man's freedom. You can only be free if I am free.

Clarence Darrow

There is no freedom on earth for those who deny freedom to others.

Elbert Hubbard

We seek peace, knowing that peace is the climate of freedom.

Dwight D. Eisenhower

The aspiration toward freedom is the most essentially human of all human manifestations.

Eric Hoffer

In the truest sense, freedom cannot be bestowed; it must be achieved.

Franklin D. Roosevelt

All free governments are managed by the combined wisdom and folly of the people.

James A. Garfield

We know the best way to enhance freedom in other lands is to demonstrate here that our democratic system is worthy of emulation.

Jimmy Carter

If it be the pleasure of Heaven that my country shall require the poor offering of my life, the victim shall be ready, at the appointed hour of sacrifice, come when that hour may. But while I do live, let me have a country that is free.

John Adams

Our institutions of freedom will not survive unless they are constantly replenished by the faith that gave them birth.

John Foster Dulles

For every man who lives without freedom, the rest of us must face the guilt.

Lillian Hellman

Freedom! No word was ever spoken that held out greater hope, demanded greater sacrifice, needed more to be nurtured, blessed more the giver, cursed more its destroyer, or came closer to being God's will on earth. And, I think that it is worth fighting for.

Omar Bradley

I know not what course others may take, but as for me, give me liberty or give me death.

Patrick Henry

Freedom is a hard-bought thing.

Paul Robeson

For what avail the plough or sail, or land or life, if freedom fail?

Ralph Waldo Emerson

Freedom is the recognition that no single person, no single authority or government has a monopoly on truth, but that every one of us put in this world has been put here for a reason and has something to offer.

Ronald Reagan

The freedom and happiness of man…are the sole objects of all legitimate government.

Thomas Jefferson

Those who expect to reap the blessings of freedom must undergo the fatigues of supporting it.

Thomas Paine

There is no power on earth equal to the power of free men and women united in the bonds of human brotherhood.

Walter P. Reuther

We must be free not because we claim freedom, but because we practice it.

William Faulkner

America is not a mere body of traders; it is a body of free men. Our greatness is built upon our freedom; it is moral, not material. We have a great ardor for gain, but we have a deeper passion for the rights of man.

Woodrow Wilson

Our greatest happiness does not depend on the condition of life in which chance has placed us, but is always the result of a good conscience, good health, occupation and freedom in all just pursuits.

Thomas Jefferson

The unity of freedom has never relied on the uniformity of opinion.

John F. Kennedy

We believe that the only whole man is a free man.

Franklin D. Roosevelt

⋆⋆⋆⋆⋆

On September 17, 1787, the Constitution of the United States of America was signed at the Constitutional Convention in Philadelphia by delegates from a dozen states. This document has guided a great nation for over two centuries, and it remains the centerpiece of American governance. Today, America faces challenges that are far different from any that our founding fathers could have imagined. Today, forces around the globe seek to terrorize our people and destroy the very fabric of our free society. Thankfully, America remains far stronger than those who seek to destroy her. No matter the cost, no matter the price, whether in dollars or blood or tears, America will prevail, in large part, because of the very freedoms that were guaranteed by the Constitution over 200 years ago.

May the sun in his course visit no land
more free, more happy, more lovely,
than this our own country.

Daniel Webster

Chapter 3

*****

COURAGE

America was not built on fear.
America was built on courage,
on imagination, and on an unbeatable
determination to do the job at hand.

Harry Truman

*D*ifficult times call for courageous measures. Running away from problems only perpetuates them; fear begets more fear, and anxiety is a poor counselor. As the Massachusetts-born philosopher Henry David Thoreau observed, "Nothing is so much to be feared as fear."

In difficult times, we learn lessons that we could have learned in no other way: Adversity visits everyone—no human being is beyond Old Man Trouble's reach. But, Old Man Trouble is not only an unwelcome guest, he is also an invaluable teacher. If we are to become mature human beings, it is our duty to learn from the inevitable hardships and heartbreaks of life.

On the pages that follow, notable Americans remind us that victory belongs to the bold. So, if you're facing a difficult situation, do the courageous thing. Courage has a way of overcoming adversity. Always has; always will.

It is impossible to win the great prizes of life without running risks.

Theodore Roosevelt

Cowards often run into the very danger they seek to avert. Don't run from anything but sin, sir, and you will be alright.

Stonewall Jackson

Bravery is the capacity to perform properly even when scared half to death.

Omar Bradley

Those who won our independence believed liberty to be the secret of happiness and courage to be the secret of liberty.

Louis D. Brandeis

If you want to conquer fear, don't sit home and think about it. Go out and get busy.

Dale Carnegie

The thing we fear we bring to pass.

Elbert Hubbard

The only thing we have to fear is fear itself.

Franklin D. Roosevelt

Stop to look fear in the face.

Eleanor Roosevelt

Courage is the price that life exacts for granting peace. The soul that knows it not knows no release from little things.

Amelia Earhart

One man with courage makes a majority.

Andrew Jackson

God grant me the courage not to give up fighting for what I think is right, even if I think it is hopeless.

Chester Nimitz

I was frightened, but I figured we needed help to get us more jobs and better education.

Rosa Parks

Valor is a gift. Those having it never know for sure whether they have it till the test comes.

Carl Sandburg

Go forth and meet the shadowy future without fear.

Henry Wadsworth Longfellow

I am not afraid of storms, for I am learning how to sail my ship.

Louisa May Alcott

Do not build up obstacles in your imagination. Difficulties must be studied and dealt with, but they must not be magnified by fear.

Norman Vincent Peale

If all Americans want is security, they can go to prison. They'll have enough to eat, a bed, and a roof over their heads. But, if an American wants to preserve his dignity and his equality as a human being, he must not bow his neck to any dictatorial government.

Dwight D. Eisenhower

Courage is doing what you're afraid to do. There can be no courage unless you're scared.

Eddie Rickenbacker

You gain strength, courage and confidence every time you look fear in the face.

Eleanor Roosevelt

Courage is grace under pressure.

Ernest Hemingway

Never take the counsel of your fears.

Andrew Jackson

When thinking won't cure fear, action will.

W. Clement Stone

Fear strikes out.

Pete Rose

Fate loves the fearless.

James Russell Lowell

For without belittling the courage with which men have died, we should not forget those acts of courage with which men have lived. A man does what he must in spite of personal consequences, in spite of obstacles and dangers and pressures, and that is the basis of all human morality.

John F. Kennedy

Courage is rarely reckless or foolish. Courage usually involves a highly realistic estimate of the odds that must be faced.

Margaret Truman

Courage is resistance to fear, mastery of fear— not the absence of fear.

Mark Twain

✮✮✮✮✮

Would you have the courage to strap yourself into a tiny capsule bolted to the top of a ten-story rocket filled to the brim with highly flammable fuel? That's exactly what the brave men and women of America's astronaut corps have done for decades. And, perhaps no member of this elite group will leave a more enduring mark on the history of modern man than Neil Armstrong, the first person to set foot on the moon.

Armstrong was born in Ohio, served his country in Korea, and became a civilian test pilot *before* he joined NASA as an astronaut in 1962. As commander of the Apollo 11, he made history when he took "one small step for a man, one giant leap for mankind." When questioned later about his fears of not returning from the moon, Neil Armstrong replied, "We planned for every negative contingency, but we expected success." And, that's a sound strategy for earthlings and spacemen alike.

If you would like to watch *your* life blast off, take this hint from NASA: plan for the worst, but don't expect it. Don't ignore your fears, but don't be ruled by them, either. And, when it comes to your expectations, visualize success. Then, like Neil Armstrong, you can confidently shoot for the moon knowing that, for men and women of courage, the sky is truly the limit.

Do the thing you fear
and the death of fear is certain.

Ralph Waldo Emerson

Chapter 4

★★★★★

HAPPINESS

"We hold these truths to be self-evident,
that all men are created equal, that they are
endowed by their Creator with certain
unalienable rights, that among these are life,
liberty, and the pursuit of happiness."

From the Declaration of Independence

The Declaration of Independence contains the words that are so familiar and so reassuring: "life, liberty, and the pursuit of happiness." And, as the American people have become increasingly prosperous, the pursuit of happiness has become one of our great national pastimes. We invest enormous amounts of time and energy in an almost endless variety of activities designed to make us happy. Enduring happiness, however, is not a commodity that can be "found"; it is an internally created condition that results from right thoughts and right behaviors.

The pursuit of happiness is a paradoxical endeavor: the more we rush after it, the more difficult it is to obtain. But, if we put matters of personal happiness aside and, instead, throw ourselves into a worthy purpose, happiness is often the byproduct. Yet, even if we are intensely involved in the pursuit of a worthy goal, happiness is not guaranteed. We must also direct the tone and quality of our thoughts.

Abraham Lincoln once observed, "Most people are about as happy as they make up their minds to be." Honest Abe understood that, for most of us, happiness is a matter of focusing our thoughts upon our blessings instead of our stumbling blocks.

American publisher Elbert Hubbard advised, "Happiness is a habit. Cultivate it." The following quotations describe time-tested methods of cultivation.

This is happiness: to be dissolved into something complete and great.

Willa Cather

True happiness is not attained through self-gratification but through fidelity to a worthy cause.

Thomas Jefferson

Happiness in this world, when it comes, comes incidentally. Make it the object of pursuit, and it leads us on a wild-goose chase and is never attained. Follow some other object, and very possibly we may find that we have caught happiness without dreaming of it.

Nathaniel Hawthorne

Happiness blossoms when you help others.

Albert Einstein

Happiness is mostly a by-product of doing what makes us feel fulfilled.

Benjamin Spock

The happiest people are those who do the most for others.

Booker T. Washington

The best way to try to cheer yourself up is to try to cheer somebody else up.

Mark Twain

The greater part of our happiness or our misery depends on our dispositions, and not on our circumstances.

Martha Washington

What we call the secret of happiness is no more a secret than our willingness to choose life.

Leo Buscaglia

Things turn out best for the people who make the best of the way things turn out.

John Wooden

We create our own happiness.

Henry David Thoreau

Happiness is the natural flower of duty.

Phillips Brooks

To fill the hour and leave no crevice…that is happiness.

Ralph Waldo Emerson

Action may not always bring happiness, but there is no happiness without action.

William James

Human happiness and moral duty are inseparably connected.

George Washington

Don't hurry. Don't worry. You're only here for a short visit. So don't forget to stop and smell the roses.

Walter Hagen

Happiness is like a cat. If you try to coax it or call it, it will avoid you. It will never come. But if you pay no attention to it and go about your business, you'll find it rubbing against your legs and jumping into your lap.

William Bennett

Happiness is a perfume that you cannot pour on others without getting a few drops on yourself.

Ralph Waldo Emerson

The best and most beautiful things in the world cannot be seen or even touched. They must be felt with the human heart.

Helen Keller

No one's happiness but my own is in my power to achieve or destroy.

Ayn Rand

When we recall the past, we usually find that it is the simplest things—not the great occasions—that, in retrospect, give off the greatest glow of happiness.

Bob Hope

Happiness doesn't depend upon who you are or what you have; it depends upon what you think.

Dale Carnegie

The mintage of wisdom is to know that rest is rust, and that real life is in love, laughter, and work.

Elbert Hubbard

Happiness lies in the joy of achievement and the thrill of creative effort.

Franklin D. Roosevelt

Happiness means having something to do and something to live for.

Fulton J. Sheen

Many persons have a wrong idea of what constitutes true happiness. It is not attained through self-gratification, but through fidelity to a worthy purpose.

Helen Keller

Though we travel the world over to find the beautiful, we must carry it with us or we find it not.

Ralph Waldo Emerson

★★★★★

Do you sincerely seek happiness? Then try a simple, fourfold approach: first, monitor your thoughts and extinguish the ones that lead to negative, self-defeating emotions. Next, associate yourself with people who are encouraging, upbeat, supportive, and honest (happiness is contagious, as is sadness). Then, find a worthy purpose for your life and throw yourself into that purpose with vigor. Finally, act responsibly (mischief and procrastination usually have unhappy consequences).

Eleanor Roosevelt observed, "Happiness is not a goal, it is a by-product," and she was right. Mrs. Roosevelt understood that when we pursue pleasure at a breakneck pace, we often do ourselves a profound disservice. But, when we wade courageously into the stream of life—with faith, with purpose, and with thanksgiving—happiness arrives quietly of its own accord.

The U. S. Constitution doesn't guarantee
happiness, only the pursuit of it.
You have to catch up with it yourself.

Ben Franklin

Chapter 5

*****

OPPORTUNITY

Every intersection on the road of life
is an opportunity.

Duke Ellington

*T*he American melting pot bubbles to the brim with opportunity. But there's a catch. To be of value, opportunities must be recognized and claimed. Ralph Waldo Emerson observed, "The world is all gates, all opportunities, strings of tension waiting to be struck." Our job is to open those gates and grasp the opportunities therein.

Because we, as Americans, have been so richly blessed, we may, on occasion, take our freedoms for granted. But, others do not. Around the world, millions of men and women dream about the day when they, too, might become United States citizens. Why? Because America is the land of new beginnings.

Each morning, as the sun rises over the Atlantic, dawn breaks upon a nation that offers its citizens freedoms and opportunities unequaled in the course of human history. Do you seek education? You can find it in America. Do you desire to worship God or speak your mind as you see fit? You can do it here. Do you dream of starting a business? In America, you can. Do you want a better life for you and your family? You can find it here. And, if something goes amiss and your dream doesn't come true, don't worry. In America, you'll be given another chance, and another, and another.

If you're lucky enough to be an American citizen, by birth or by choice, you are surrounded by more opportunities than you can count. So do yourself a favor. Start counting them anyway and then start claiming them…today.

Never surrender opportunity to security.

Branch Rickey

Opportunity is missed because it is dressed in overalls and looks like work.

Thomas Edison

This time, like all times, is a very good one if we only know what to do with it.

Ralph Waldo Emerson

We are confronted with insurmountable opportunities.

Walt Kelly

Twenty years from now you will be more disappointed by the things you didn't do than by the ones you did do. So throw off the bowlines. Sail away from the safe harbor. Catch the trade winds in your sails. Explore. Dream. Discover.

Mark Twain

Rather than face the mere possibility of pain, we remain inactive, or we do something easier than we should attempt. This is illogical, of course.

Dorthea Brande

All the lovely sentiments in the world weigh less than a single lovely action.

James Russell Lowell

He started to sing as he tackled the thing that couldn't be done, and he did it.

Edgar A. Guest

God had infinite time to give us. He cut it up into a near succession of new mornings, and, with each therefore, a new idea, new inventions, and new applications.

Ralph Waldo Emerson

You may live in an imperfect world, but the frontiers are not closed and the doors are not all shut.

Maxwell Maltz

Opportunity is infinite.

Mark Victor Hansen

Life is kicking you in the britches all the time, if you only know it.

Katherine Anne Porter

Every day is a new opportunity. That's the way life is, with a new game every day.

Bob Feller

Whether it's the best of times or the worst of times, it's the only time you've got.

Art Buchwald

We are continually faced by great opportunities brilliantly disguised as insoluble problems.

Lee Iacocca

Each day the world is born anew for him who takes it rightly.

James Russell Lowell

A problem is an opportunity in work clothes.

Henry J. Kaiser, Jr.

No matter what our job description, we all work for ourselves. Accordingly, our opportunities are exactly as big as we make them.

J. R. Freeman

Men are not prisoners of fate, but only prisoners of their own minds.

Franklin D. Roosevelt

Opportunity does not knock, it presents itself when you beat down the door.

Raymond Chandler

Dreams never hurt anybody who kept working right behind the dream to make as much of it come true as possible.

F. W. Woolworth

One can never consent to creep when one has the impulse to soar.

Helen Keller

If one is lucky, a solitary fantasy can totally transform one million realities.

Maya Angelou

There is always room at the top.

Daniel Webster

Hitch your wagon to a star.

Ralph Waldo Emerson

Are you disappointed, discouraged and discontented with your present level of success? Are you secretly dissatisfied with your present status? Do you want to become a better and more beautiful person than you are today? Would you like to be able to really learn how to be proud of yourself and still not lose genuine humility? Then start dreaming! It's possible! You can become the person you have always wanted to be!

Robert Schuller

I like dreams of the future better than the history of the past.

Thomas Jefferson

I can't believe that there are any heights that can't be scaled by a man who knows the secrets of making dreams come true. This special secret, it seems to me, can be summarized in four C's. They are curiosity, confidence, courage, and constancy, and the greatest of all is confidence.

Walt Disney

✯✯✯✯✯

Isidore Baline (1888-1989) was born in Russia in May of 1888. Four years later, he immigrated with his family to America. Isidore grew up in a poor New York City neighborhood. For a time, he made his living as a singing waiter, but he found his true calling in 1907 when he began writing songs. Along the way, Isidore changed his name to Irving Berlin, and, in 1911, he published his first hit: *Alexander's Ragtime Band*. His two greatest classics are *God Bless America* and *White Christmas*.

Berlin once observed, "Life is ten percent how you make it and ninety percent how you take it." He understood that in life, attitude is everything. As a relative newcomer to America, Berlin appreciated his opportunities, and he made the most of them. When success arrived, he was more than willing to share it. In 1939, when his song *God Bless America* became wildly popular, Berlin donated his royalties from the song to the Boy Scouts and Girl Scouts.

If you've become caught up in the daily grind, slow down, compose your thoughts, count all of your blessings, and remember the advice of the Russian immigrant who wrote *God Bless America*. Then, get busy turning your dreams into reality. In America, opportunities are endless, but the competition is stiff, and success doesn't happen without effort. The best way to make sure that your dreams come true is to keep working until they do.

✯✯✯✯✯

If one advances confidently in the direction
of his dreams, and endeavors to live the life
which he has imagined, he will meet
with success unexpected in common hours.

Henry David Thoreau

Chapter 6

★★★★★

WORK

Work as if you were to live a hundred years.
Pray as if you were to die tomorrow.

Ben Franklin

*I*n America, dreams indeed come true for those who are willing to do the following: 1. Work hard and smart, and 2. Keep working hard and smart. American educator Booker T. Washington observed, "Nothing ever comes to one that is worth having except as a result of hard work." Now, almost a century after Mr. Washington's death, little has changed. America is still a land of opportunities, but not a land of guarantees.

Thomas Edison became one of America's most original and productive inventors despite the fact that his formal education was limited to a mere three months. When questioned about his success, Edison spoke these familiar words: "Genius is one percent inspiration and ninety-nine percent perspiration." Edison and his associates invented the first practical incandescent light, the phonograph, motion-picture equipment, and a thousand other patented devices. These impressive accomplishments came not so much from isolated creative genius as from endless hours of old-fashioned, shoulder-to-the-wheel hard work.

Americans who sincerely seek better lives for themselves and their families must remember that the secret to success in America is, in large part, a willingness to get the job done and to get it done now.

As men and women of character and of faith in the soundness of democratic methods, we must work like dogs to justify that faith.

Dwight D. Eisenhower

Diligence is the mother of good luck, and God gives all things to industry. Then plough deep while sluggards sleep, and you shall have corn to sell and to keep.

Ben Franklin

It isn't enough to talk about peace. One must believe in it. And it isn't enough to believe in it. One must work at it.

Eleanor Roosevelt

What we need are patriots who express their faith in their country by working to improve it.

Hubert H. Humphrey

If the power to do hard work is not talent, it is the best possible substitute for it.

James A. Garfield

The road to happiness lies in two simple principles: find what it is that interests you and that you can do well, and when you find it, put your whole soul into it—every bit of energy and ambition and natural ability you have.

John D. Rockefeller

The American, by nature, is optimistic. He is experimental, an inventor and a builder who builds best when called upon to build greatly.

John F. Kennedy

To love what you do and feel that it matters— how could anything be more fun?

Katherine Graham

No one can really pull you up very high; you lose your grip on the rope. But on your own two feet, you can climb mountains.

Louis D. Brandeis

The best prize that life offers is the chance to work hard at work worth doing.

Theodore Roosevelt

I never did anything worth doing by accident, nor did any of my inventions come by accident. They came by work.

Thomas Edison

They say good things come to those who wait.
I believe that good things come to those who work.

Wilt Chamberlain

The harder you work, the harder it is for you
to surrender.

Vince Lombardi

I've always believed that if you put in the work,
the results will come.

Michael Jordan

The key to my success? Understanding that
there's no free lunch.

Lou Holtz

The best thing I've learned in life is that things have to be worked for. There's no magic in making a winning team, but there's plenty of work.

Knute Rockne

Nothing will work unless you do.

John Wooden

You can have anything you want if you're willing to pay the price.

Eddie Robinson

I have never heard of anyone stumbling on something while sitting down.

Charles Kettering

Do your work with your whole heart, and you will succeed—there is so little competition.

Elbert Hubbard

Nothing is particularly hard if you divide it into small steps.

Henry Ford

Talent is only a starting point in this business. You've got to keep on working that talent.

Irving Berlin

My success just evolved from working hard at the business at hand each day.

Johnny Carson

Everything worthwhile, everything of any value, has a price. The price is effort.

Loretta Young

I don't know anything about luck. I've never banked on it, and I'm afraid of people who do. Luck to me is something else: hard work and realizing what is opportunity and what isn't.

Lucille Ball

★★★★★

She was born Erma Louise Fiste, but she is best known by her married name, Erma Bombeck. Her syndicated columns and television commentaries entertained millions of Americans. Bombeck was a very funny lady, but when it came to her work and her talent, she was quite serious. Shortly before her death in 1996, Erma wrote, "When I stand before God at the end of my life, I would hope that I have not a single bit of talent left and could say, 'Lord, I used everything you gave me.'"

All of us are blessed with talents that are ours to nurture—or not—as we see fit. The process of transforming natural ability into desired results requires work…and lots of it. Often, it seems easier to ignore gifts than to do the work of cultivating them, but cultivate we must. To do otherwise is to squander a precious gift from God.

Erma Bombeck used her talent to the full, and so should we. Time is short, the needs are great, and the Giver is watching.

Hard work beats all the tonics and
vitamins in the world.

Harland Sanders

Chapter 7

*****

PERSEVERANCE

It is part of the American character
to consider nothing as desperate,
to surmount every difficulty
by resolution and ingenuity.

Thomas Jefferson

*A*merica was not built by quitters. To the contrary, the men and women who built this nation were resolute in their determination to succeed, and we should be, too. John Quincy Adams observed, "Courage and perseverance have a magical talisman, before which difficulties disappear and obstacles vanish into thin air." His words still ring true. When we attack our problems courageously—and keep attacking them—our successes *seem* magical, but they are not magic—they are the result of endurance and will.

Do you seek a "magical talisman" that will help ensure that you earn the rewards you desire from life? If so, don't go looking in the local magic shop; instead look inside yourself and bring forth the inner strength to keep working even when you'd rather quit. Find the courage to stand firm in the face of adversity. Don't back up and don't back down. Because, as John Quincy Adams correctly observed, courage and perseverance have a way of making problems disappear…unless you disappear first.

Always bear in mind that your own resolution
to succeed is more important than any one thing.

Abraham Lincoln

Diligence overcomes difficulties; sloth makes
them.

Ben Franklin

That which we persist in doing becomes
easier—not that the nature of the task has changed,
but our ability has increased.

Ralph Waldo Emerson

Never give up and never give in.

Hubert H. Humphrey

To get where you want to go, you must keep on keeping on.

Norman Vincent Peale

There is no royal road to anything. Do one thing at a time and all things in succession. That which grows slowly, endures.

Josiah Gilbert Holland

We can do anything we want to do if we stick to it long enough.

Helen Keller

When you get into a tight place and everything goes against you, till it seems as though you could not hang on a minute longer, never give up then, for that is just the place and the time the tide will turn.

Harriet Beecher Stowe

It's not that I'm so smart; it's just that I stay with problems longer.

Albert Einstein

Nothing in the world can take the place of persistence. Talent will not; genius will not; education will not. Persistence and determination alone are omnipotent.

Calvin Coolidge

There is no chance, no destiny, no fate, that can hinder or control the firm resolve of a determined soul.

Ella Wheeler Wilcox

Perseverance is a great element of success. If you only knock long enough and loud enough at the gate, you are sure to wake up somebody.

Henry Wadsworth Longfellow

If you run into a wall, don't turn around and give up. Figure out how to climb it, go through it, or work around it.

Michael Jordan

My motto was always to keep swinging. Whether I was in a slump or feeling badly or having trouble off the field, the only thing to do was keep swinging.

Hank Aaron

You just can't beat the person who never gives up.

Babe Ruth

You have to find something that you love enough to be able to take risks, jump over the hurdles, and break through the brick walls that are always going to be placed in front of you. If you don't have that kind of feeling for what it is you're doing, you'll stop at the first giant hurdle.

George Lucas

Effort only fully releases its reward after a person refuses to quit.

Napoleon Hill

I am not the smartest or most talented person in the world, but I succeeded because I kept going, and going, and going.

Sylvester Stallone

Just don't give up trying to do what you really want to do. Where there is love and inspiration, I don't think you can go wrong.

Ella Fitzgerald

Keep your mind on your objective, and persist until you succeed.

W. Clement Stone

I never felt like throwing in the towel. It took seven years of auditions until I started learning how to perform. It was discouraging, but I never quit because I love what I do.

Tony Bennett

One may walk over the highest mountain one step at a time.

John Wanamaker

I have not yet begun to fight.

John Paul Jones

Big shots are only little shots who kept shooting.

Harvey Mackay

It takes twenty years to make an overnight success.

Eddie Cantor

Success seems to be connected with action. Successful men keep moving. They make mistakes, but they don't quit.

Conrad Hilton

I walk slowly, but I never walk backwards.

Abraham Lincoln

I think and think for months and years. Ninety-nine times, the conclusion is false. The hundredth time, I am right.

Albert Einstein

★★★★★

Her real name was Gladys Mary Smith and she was born in Canada, but she became "America's sweetheart" in the early days of motion pictures. She was Mary Pickford, and in 1919, along with Charlie Chaplin, Douglas Fairbanks, and D.W. Griffith, she formed United Artists Corporation, a Hollywood powerhouse.

Miss Pickford had a simple yet powerful formula for success: She said, "This thing we call 'failure' is not falling down, but staying down." Pickford understood that nothing succeeds like persistence.

From time to time, life knocks all of us down. But in America, it is up to *us* to decide whether or not we stay down. May God bless a nation wise enough to offer second chances *and* a people wise enough to take them.

Don't give up at halftime.
Concentrate on winning the second half.

Bear Bryant

Chapter 8

*****

CREATIVITY
AND
INNOVATION

The creative impulse is never satisfied.
It is self-expression…the basic need to make
evident one's deepest feelings about life.

Aaron Copland

*F*reedom breeds creativity, and more freedom breeds more creativity. Perhaps that helps explain why the creative spirit covers the American landscape from the mountains to the prairies, and from the Atlantic to the Pacific. Theologian Reinhold Niebuhr observed, "It is better to create than to be learned; creating is the true essence of life." And, he might have added that life in the good old USA is made rich by the boundless creativity of the American people.

Do you have a dream? Dream it here. Do you have a song in your heart? Step up on stage and sing it here. Do you have a story to tell? Write it. A business idea? Start your business in the garage…like Henry Ford (or, for that matter, like Hewlett and Packard). America loves its creators, its innovators, its tinkerers, its builders, and its dreamers.

Entertainment pioneer Walt Disney, who also started *his* business in a garage, advised, "If you can dream it, you can do it. " And, his words have never been more true than they are today. So, if you feel the urge to create something new out of nothing more than your own creative genius, you've come to the right place. In America, there's nothing holding you back *except* the quality of your idea and your willingness to see it through…and, perhaps, a messy garage.

A man must consider what rich realm he abdicates when he becomes a conformist.

Ralph Waldo Emerson

Towering genius disdains a beaten path.

Abraham Lincoln

If a man write a better book, preach a better sermon, or make a better mousetrap than his neighbor, though he build his house in the woods, the world will make a beaten path to his door.

Ralph Waldo Emerson

Follow the path of the unsafe, independent thinker. Expose your ideas to the dangers of controversy. Speak your mind and fear less the label of crackpot than the stigma of conformity. And on issues that seem important to you, stand up and be counted at any cost.

Thomas J. Watson

Creativity is a highfalutin word for the work I have to do between now and Tuesday.

Ray Kroc

In creating, the only hard part is to begin.

James Russell Lowell

When I started thinking "outside the box," it revolutionized my business.

J. R. Freeman

One of the greatest necessities in America is to discover creative solitude.

Carl Sandburg

If you want to succeed, you should strike out on new paths rather than travel the worn paths of accepted success.

John D. Rockefeller

To be an innovator, you can't be worried about making mistakes.

Julius Erving

Innovation is more than a new method. It is a new view of the universe.

Peter Drucker

The world is moving so fast these days that the man who says it can't be done is generally interrupted by someone doing it.

Elbert Hubbard

Millions saw the apple fall, but Newton was the one to ask why.

Bernard Baruch

Go around asking a lot of foolish questions and taking chances. Only through curiosity can we discover opportunities, and only by gambling can we take advantage of them.

Clarence Birdseye

Over the years, I have learned that every significant invention has several characteristics. By definition it must be startling, unexpected, and must come to a world that is not prepared for it. If the world were prepared for it, it would not be much of an invention.

Edwin Land

My work, my life, must be in the spirit of a little child seeking only to know the truth and follow it.

George Washington Carver

A creative life is so much more important than a structured, shadowed existence.

Doc Pomus

I like nonsense, it wakes up the brain cells. Fantasy is a necessary ingredient in living. It's a way of looking at life through the wrong end of the telescope, which is what I do. And that enables you to laugh at life's realities.

Dr. Seuss

Create and be true to yourself and rely only on your own good taste.

Duke Ellington

Creative people have to be fed from the divine source.

Johnny Cash

Man, surrounded by facts, permitting himself no surprise, no intuitive flash, no great hypothesis, no risk, is in a locked cell.

Lillian Smith

No artist is ahead of his time. He is his time; it is just that others are behind the times.

Martha Graham

I'm always thinking about creating. My future starts when I wake up every morning. Every day I find something creative to do with my life.

Miles Davis

I prefer to go in my own direction and let someone follow me.

Roger Miller

Adhere to your own act, and congratulate yourself if you have done something strange and extravagant, and broken the monotony of a decorous age.

Ralph Waldo Emerson

The man who has no imagination has no wings.

Muhammad Ali

You have to allow a certain amount of time in which you are doing nothing in order to have things occur to you, to let your mind think.

Mortimer Adler

When the spirit of child's play enters into the creative process, it's a wonderful force and something to be nurtured.

Joni Mitchell

Albert Einstein was an American, not by birth, but by choice (he became a naturalized citizen in 1940). It goes without saying that Einstein's theories redefined the way scientists understand our universe. But how, pray tell, did the world's most memorable absent-minded professor arrive at his revolutionary theories? By paying less attention to the prevailing wisdom of the day and more attention to his own intuition. Einstein observed, "The intellect has little to do on the road to discovery. There comes a leap in consciousness, call it intuition or what you will, and the solution comes to you and you don't know how or why."

Would you like to add a dash of creative genius to your life? Follow the Einstein method and trust your intuition. The small still voice inside is seldom wrong. Listen for it and trust it.

Be a Columbus to whole new continents
and worlds within you, opening new
channels, not of trade, but of thought.

Henry David Thoreau

Chapter 9

*****

ATTITUDE

Keep your face to the sunshine
and you cannot see the shadow.

Helen Keller

At the age of two, she was stricken with what 19th-century doctors called "brain fever." When the illness abated, Helen Keller was left deaf and blind. Keller might have been excused for having a sour attitude about life, but she did not give in to the paralysis of bitterness and despair. Instead, with the help of an extraordinary teacher named Anne Sullivan, young Helen learned to communicate and quickly embraced education. Eventually, Keller graduated *cum laude* from Radcliffe, and then went on to become a noted American writer, lecturer, and advocate for the handicapped.

Keller once observed, "When we do the best we can, we never know what miracles await." That's exactly the kind of red-white-and-blue optimism that made America the greatest nation on earth. A positive attitude is as American as mom and apple pie…as the following quotations clearly demonstrate.

Believe you can and you are halfway there.

Theodore Roosevelt

An inexhaustible good nature is one of the most precious gifts of heaven.

Washington Irving

You cannot always control what goes on outside. But you can always control what goes on inside.

Wayne Dyer

The greatest discovery of my generation is that man can alter his life simply by altering his attitude.
William James

A positive attitude will have positive results because attitudes are contagious.
Zig Ziglar

There is very little difference in people, but that little difference makes a big difference. The little difference is attitude.
W. Clement Stone

We find in life exactly what we put in.
Ralph Waldo Emerson

Life reflects your own thoughts back to you.

Napoleon Hill

Your state of mind creates your state of results.

Mark Victor Hansen

Success is a state of mind. If you want success, start thinking of yourself as a success.

Joyce Brothers

Games aren't necessarily won by teams with the best players. They're won by teams with the best attitude.

George Allen

Even if you're not number one, you should have the attitude that you're number one.

Joe Paterno

Ability is what you're capable of doing. Motivation determines what you do. Attitude determines how well you do it.

Lou Holtz

A strong positive attitude will create more miracles than any wonder drug.

Patricia Neal

The only disability in life is a bad attitude.

Scott Hamilton

If you have a negative thought, don't waste hours thinking about it. Simply direct yourself to something positive, and keep repeating the positive until you eliminate the negative.

Tina Louise

I was always dumb enough to think I could do anything, and I got lucky sometimes and did it.

Willie Nelson

★★★★★

In 1919, Conrad Hilton paid $5,000 for a small Texas hotel and began acquiring more properties. Over the years, his name became synonymous with quality and service. He even purchased New York's famed Waldorf-Astoria and made it a crowned jewel in his chain. Hilton's advice for life was as expansive as Texas. He said, "Think big. Act big. Dream big."

If you've been afraid to dream big dreams, it's time to reconsider. Good things *do* happen to good people, but the best things are usually reserved for those who expect the best and plan for it. So, put the self-fulfilling prophecy to work for you, and start dreaming in Technicolor. And, remember that since dreams often do come true, you might as well make your dreams Texas-sized. Just like Conrad Hilton.

★★★★★

Your attitude, not your aptitude,
will determine your altitude.

Zig Ziglar

Chapter 10

*****

GENEROSITY

I hope ever to see America among
the foremost nations in examples
of justice and generosity.

George Washington

*A*mericans have been richly blessed, and they are quick to share their blessings. Whether the needs are here at home or far away, the response is the same: Americans care enough to help.

Over a century ago, novelist Herman Melville observed, "We cannot live only for ourselves. A thousand fibers connect us with our fellow men." Nothing has changed since then. The world is still a difficult place where too many people struggle for the bare necessities of life. And so it is only proper that a prosperous people would give generously to those who are unable to help themselves.

Have you been blessed with more material possessions than you can use? If so, share the wealth. This nation and this world desperately needs an army of generous Americans…and Uncle Sam wants you!

Turning our eyes to other nations, our great desire is to see our brethren of the human race secured in the blessings enjoyed by ourselves, and advancing in knowledge, in freedom, and in social happiness.

Andrew Jackson

No person was ever honored for what he received. Honor has been the reward for what he gave.

Calvin Coolidge

Would we hold liberty, we must have charity; charity to others, charity to ourselves....

Learned Hand

When you cease to contribute, you begin to die.

Eleanor Roosevelt

The happiest people are those who do the most for others.

Booker T. Washington

It is one of the most beautiful compensations of this life that no man can sincerely try to help another without helping himself.

Ralph Waldo Emerson

I must admit that I personally measure success in terms of the contributions an individual makes to her or his fellow human beings.

Margaret Mead

The reward of a good deed is to have done it.

Elbert Hubbard

If you haven't any charity in your heart, you have the worst kind of heart trouble.

Bob Hope

We must not slacken our efforts to do good to all, especially to those with needs that will not be met if we fail in our common task of service to humanity.

Danny Thomas

The more good I do, the more money comes back to me.

Ted Turner

There is a very real relationship, both quantitatively and qualitatively, between what you contribute and what you get out of this world.

Oscar Hammerstein

He climbs the highest who helps another up.

Zig Ziglar

What is serving God? 'Tis doing good to man.

Poor Richard's Almanac

Give what you have. To someone, it may be better than you dare to think.

Henry Wadsworth Longfellow

Look up and not down. Look forward and not back. Look out and not in, and lend a hand.

Edward Everett Hale

The highest test of the civilization of any race is in its willingness to extend a helping hand to the less fortunate.

Booker T. Washington

We find in life exactly what we put in it.

Ralph Waldo Emerson

Assistance to the weak makes one strong. Oppression of the unfortunate makes one weak.

Booker T. Washington

★★★★★

In the 1950's and 60's, Danny Thomas was one of America's favorite TV comedians. But, his road to the top was not always easy. In fact, Thomas almost abandoned his career before it really began.

As a young man, Danny Thomas became so discouraged with the direction of his professional life that he made the decision to quit show business altogether. But, before quitting, he prayed a final prayer of desperation to Saint Jude, the patron saint of those in need. The very next day, Thomas received a job offer that turned his career around. Eventually, he went on to become the beloved star of the TV's *Make Room for Daddy* (and a co-producer of the classic *Andy Griffith Show*).

As a way of giving something back, Thomas endowed the St. Jude Children's Research Hospital in Memphis, Tennessee. And because of the work at St. Jude's, countless young lives have been saved. Thomas said, "Success has nothing to do with what you gain or accomplish for yourself. It's what you do for others that counts." And, that's wonderful advice from a man whose life bore testimony to his words.

From what we get, we can make a living;
what we give, however, makes a life.

Arthur Ashe

Chapter 11

★★★★★

EDUCATION

Next in importance to freedom and justice
is popular education, without which neither
freedom nor justice can be permanently
maintained.

James A. Garfield

*W*hat is education? Education defies simple definition because it occurs in so many different locations and on so many different levels. Of course, education takes place inside the classroom, but it also takes place in countless other settings. We learn from teachers, parents, coaches, bosses, peers and books. Sometimes, wisdom comes from observation; other times only from bitter experience.

Perhaps the best definition of education was proposed by American philanthropist George Peabody. He said, "Education is a debt from present to future generations." In this chapter, we consider the implications of that debt, along with intelligent plans for repayment.

The education of a man is never completed until he dies.

Robert E. Lee

At the desk where I sit, I have learned one great truth. The answer for all our national problems, the answer for all the problems of the world, is summarized in a single word. That word is "education."

Lyndon Baines Johnson

Our progress as a nation can be no swifter than our progress in education. The human mind is our fundamental resource.

John F. Kennedy

Education is not a preparation for life; education is life itself.

John Dewey

Education is not given for the purpose of earning a living; it's learning what to do with a living after you've earned it.

Abraham Lincoln

Genius without education is like silver in the mine.

Ben Franklin

America's future will be determined by the home and the school. The child becomes largely what it is taught; hence, we must watch what we teach it and how we live before it.

Jane Addams

Out of the public schools grows the greatness of a nation.

Mark Twain

The growth of the human mind is still high adventure, in many ways the highest adventure on earth.

Norman Cousins

Invest in yourself, in your education. There's nothing better.

Sylvia Porter

Education is the mother of leadership.

Wendell Willkie

The only thing more expensive than education is ignorance.

Ben Franklin

I learned the importance of self-education. Once you realize that the learning is up to you, you have the right attitude to succeed in school and beyond.

Tony Bennett

Education is the key to unlock the golden door of freedom.

Thomas Jefferson

Education is hanging on until you've caught on.

Robert Frost

The things taught in schools and colleges are not an education, but a means to an education.

Ralph Waldo Emerson

Education's purpose is to replace an empty mind with an open one.

Malcolm Forbes

Apply yourself. Get all the education you can, but then do something. Don't just stand there; make it happen.

Lee Iacocca

Not the school, nor the teachers, but the student is the preponderant factor in education.

James Weldon Johnson

The central task of education is to implant a will and facility for learning; it should produce not learned but learning people.

Eric Hoffer

★★★★★

Education should never be restricted to our schools and colleges. In fact, the most important part of any person's educational experience should occur *outside* the ivy-covered halls of academia. To be successful in this rapidly changing world, one must make learning a lifetime endeavor.

Mel Tormé, co-composer of "The Christmas Song," fashioned a six-decade career as one of America's most admired popular singers. But, things weren't always easy for Tormé. In fact, in the late sixties, business was so slow for Mel that he reportedly considered giving up show business altogether and becoming an airline pilot. Instead, he buckled down, kept improving his craft, and eventually rebuilt his career. Mr. Tormé observed, "A career and a life should be a giant learning curve and a work in progress." And, of course, he was right.

The next time you're tempted to rest on *your* laurels, remember the man they called, "The Velvet Fog," and remember that as long as you're alive, *your* life is a work in progress. So why not be like Mel and create a masterpiece?

All of life is a constant education.

Eleanor Roosevelt

Chapter 12

* * * * *

LEADERSHIP

If we falter in our leadership we may endanger
the peace of the world, and we shall surely
endanger the welfare of the nation.

Harry Truman

$\mathcal{H}$arry S Truman was the plain-spoken American president who uttered the now-familiar phrase, "If you can't stand the heat, get out of the kitchen." And, he spoke from experience. As commander-in-chief during the waning days of World War II, the feisty Truman faced many tough decisions, and he never dodged them. Instead, he followed the advice of fellow Democrat Andrew Jackson, who said, "Take time to deliberate; but when the time for action arrives, stop thinking and go ahead."

Leadership is not a popularity contest. Far from it. Genuine leadership often requires tough decisions; tough decisions, by their definition, are displeasing to some. But, effective leaders are willing to sacrifice popularity for results. Period.

If you desire a position of leadership, be forewarned: the day will come—and sooner than you expect—when you will be faced with a tough, unpopular decision. When that day arrives, you have a choice to make: you can either do the right thing or the easy thing. Do the right thing. After all, every kitchen heats up on occasion, so you might as well get used to it. And, the best way to get used to a warm kitchen is to hang in there and take the heat, knowing that every kitchen, in time, cools down. And so will yours.

It takes leaders with vision to help people with dreams.

Hubert H. Humphrey

The very essence of leadership is that you have to have a vision. You can't blow an uncertain trumpet.

Theodore Hesburgh

Leadership is the knack of getting somebody to do something you want done because he wants to do it.

Dwight D. Eisenhower

Sandwich every bit of criticism between two heavy layers of praise.

Mary Kay Ash

I cannot trust a man to control others who cannot control himself.

Robert E. Lee

We need to learn to set our course by the stars and not by the lights of every passing ship.

Omar Bradley

When placed in charge, take control.

Norman Schwarzkopf

Effective leadership is visionary leadership.
Mark Victor Hansen

Outstanding leaders go out of their way to boost the self-esteem of their personnel. If people believe in themselves, it's amazing what they can accomplish.

Sam Walton

Motivation is everything. You can do the work of two people, but you can't be two people. Instead, you have to inspire the next guy down the line and get him to inspire his people.

Lee Iacocca

If you're ridin' ahead of the herd, take a look back every now and then to make sure it's still there.

Will Rogers

Leadership, like coaching, is fighting for the hearts and souls of men, and getting them to believe in you.

Eddie Robinson

Nobody wants to follow somebody who doesn't know where he's going.

Joe Namath

Life is far more flexible than it seems to those who are unwilling to act.

Dorothea Brand

You cannot run a business, or anything else, on a theory.

Harold S. Geneen

Leadership comes from competence. Leadership is by example, not by talk.

Bill Walsh

To be a truly great leader, you must give of yourself. You must convey a vision of partnership that you not only care about the people who work for you, but think it's important that they're successful, too.

Rick Pitino

Effective leadership is putting first things first. Effective management is discipline, carrying it out.

Stephen Covey

Leadership begins with self-knowledge. Life decisions can be good decisions only if they reflect your own personal bedrock.

Vince Lombardi

In his day, he was the winningest coach in college football, and in the state of Alabama he is still an icon, almost two full decades after his death. He was the legendary Paul "Bear" Bryant, and his advice for life was simple. Coach Bryant said, "In a crisis, don't hide behind anything or anybody. They're going to find you anyway."

If you seek to be an effective leader, prepare yourself for the crises that, from time to time, visit every organization. And when Old Man Trouble knocks on your door, open the door and face him square on. As Bear Bryant would be quick to point out, there's no future in ducking your responsibilities. Besides, when you look Old Man Trouble straight in the eye, he usually blinks, and when he does, you win…and so does your team.

Have a vision. Be demanding.

Colin Powell

Chapter 13

★★★★★

ALL-PURPOSE ADVICE

He that won't be counseled can't be helped.

Ben Franklin

*A*merica is a land of plenty, and that includes giving advice. Everywhere we turn, or so it seems, we find an ample supply of recommendations, instructions, suggestions, tips, hints, insights, opinions, communications, memoranda, warnings, appeals to better judgment, bright ideas, and words to the wise. From the self-help section of the local bookstore to the Dear Abby column in the local newspaper, we Americans gobble up advice and then keep gobbling. Hopefully, most of this advice has two overriding characteristics: first, that it is helpful, and second, that it is acted upon. With that thought in mind, we conclude with an abbreviated assortment of admonitions from an assemblage of astute Americans. Enjoy, and God bless this great land!

Stay interested in everything and everybody. It keeps you young.

Marie T. Freeman

It is not the years in your life but the life in your years that counts.

Adlai E. Stevenson

I learned to love the journey, not the destination. I learned that this is not a dress rehearsal, and that today is the only guarantee you get.

Anna Quindlen

Life is available to anyone, no matter what age. All you have to do is grab it.

Art Carney

A long life may not be good enough, but a good life is long enough.

Ben Franklin

Don't go to your grave with a life unused.

Bobby Bowden

Time is the coin of your life. It is the only coin you have, and only you can determine how it will be spent. Be careful lest you let other people spend it for you.

Carl Sandburg

The longer I live, the more beautiful life becomes.

Frank Lloyd Wright

I will not live my life. I will not spend my life. I will invest my life.

Helen Keller

Develop interest in life as you see it; in people, things, literature, music—the world is so rich, simply throbbing with rich treasures, beautiful souls, and interesting people. Forget yourself.

Henry Miller

The thing to remember when traveling is that the trail is the thing, not the end of the trail. Travel too fast and you miss all that you are traveling for.

Louis L'Amour

Assume responsibility for the quality of your own life.

Norman Cousins

The more you praise and celebrate your life, the more there is in life to celebrate.

Oprah Winfrey

God has given each one of us approximately 25,000 days on this earth. I truly believe He has something very specific in mind: 8,300 days to sleep, 8,300 to work, 8,300 to give, live, play, pray, and love one another.

Quincy Jones

Life isn't a matter of milestones but of moments.

Rose Kennedy

Far better it is to dare mighty things, to win glorious triumphs, even though checkered by failure, than to take rank with those poor spirits who neither enjoy much nor suffer much, because they live in the gray twilight that knows neither victory nor defeat.

Theodore Roosevelt

We are here just for a spell and then pass on. So get a few laughs and do the best you can. Live your life so that whenever you lose, you are ahead.

Will Rogers

The greatest use of a life is to spend it for something that will outlast it.

William James

I would rather be ashes than dust. I would rather that my spark should burn out in a brilliant blaze than it should be stifled by dry rot. The proper function of man is to live, not to exist.

Jack London

To me there are three things everyone should do every day. Number one is to laugh. Number two is to spend some time in thought. Number three is to have your emotions move you to tears. If you laugh, think, and cry, that's a heck of a day.

Jim Valvano

Our attitude towards life determines life's attitude towards us.

Earl Nightingale

I promise to keep on living as though I expected to live forever. Nobody grows old by merely living a number of years. People grow old by deserting their ideals. Years may wrinkle the skin, but to give up wrinkles the soul.

Douglas MacArthur

Life is a great big canvas, and you should throw all the paint on it you can.

Danny Kaye

All of us tend to put off living. We are all dreaming of some magical rose garden over the horizon instead of enjoying the roses that are blooming outside our windows today.

Dale Carnegie

Life is a succession of moments. To live each one is to succeed.

Corita Kent

Life shrinks or expands in proportion to one's courage.

Anaïs Nin

Consider the lilies of the field. Look at the fuzz on a baby's ear. Read in the backyard with the sun on your face. Learn to be happy. And think of life as a terminal illness, because, if you do, you will live it with joy and passion, as it ought to be lived.

Anna Quindlen

Make each day your masterpiece.

John Wooden